HEARTS AND FLORALS

BOOK 1

A COLORING BOOK FOR ADULTS AND TEENS

Marie Kaye

INTRODUCTION

Thanks for entering into this adventure in coloring. I am looking forward to sharing my love and passion for artistic coloring with you.

I created all of the images in this book by hand using my own personal collection of photos taken by myself as inspiration. I then used various symmetry software tools to complete the overall designs you see here.

Although the images are copyrighted, as the buyer of this book, please feel free to copy them for your personal use. If you choose to do so, this will keep the book new and ready for use. Some folks prefer to color on a heavier paper so that the color from marker pens will not bleed through the paper. I'll often color on 80lb paper.

Each image is on only one side of the page, the reverse side being left blank. If you'd rather color right inside the book, I'd recommend using a thin piece of cardboard behind your page, just to protect the next image from any color bleeding through to the next page, especially if you plan to use marker pens for coloring. This will keep all your images clean for you to work on.

The designs are suitable from beginning to advanced students. The important thing is . . . HAVE FUN!

Don't forget to check out my other books in the HEARTS AND FLORALS series. I am dedicated to producing these designs for you.

- Marie Kaye

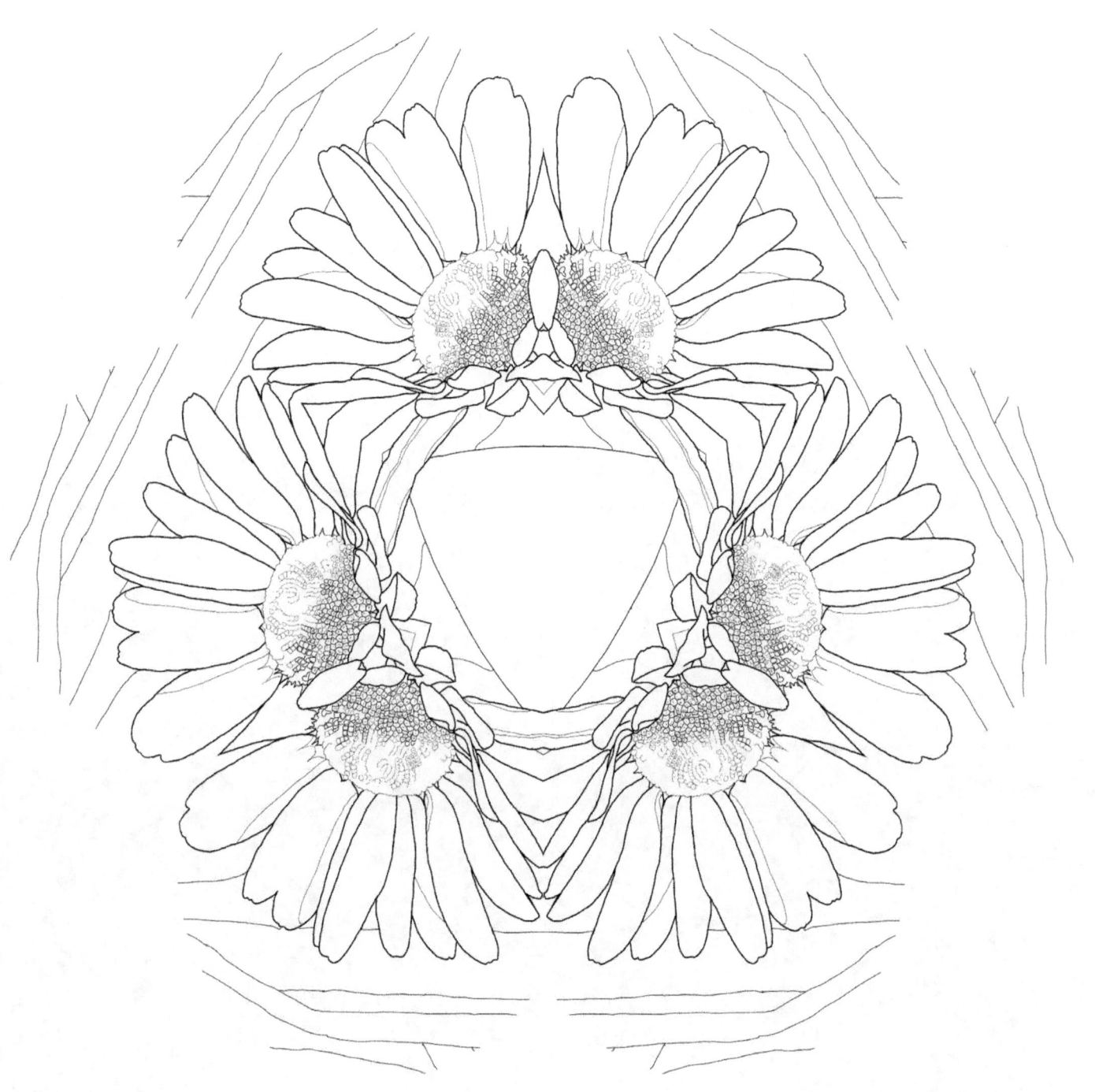

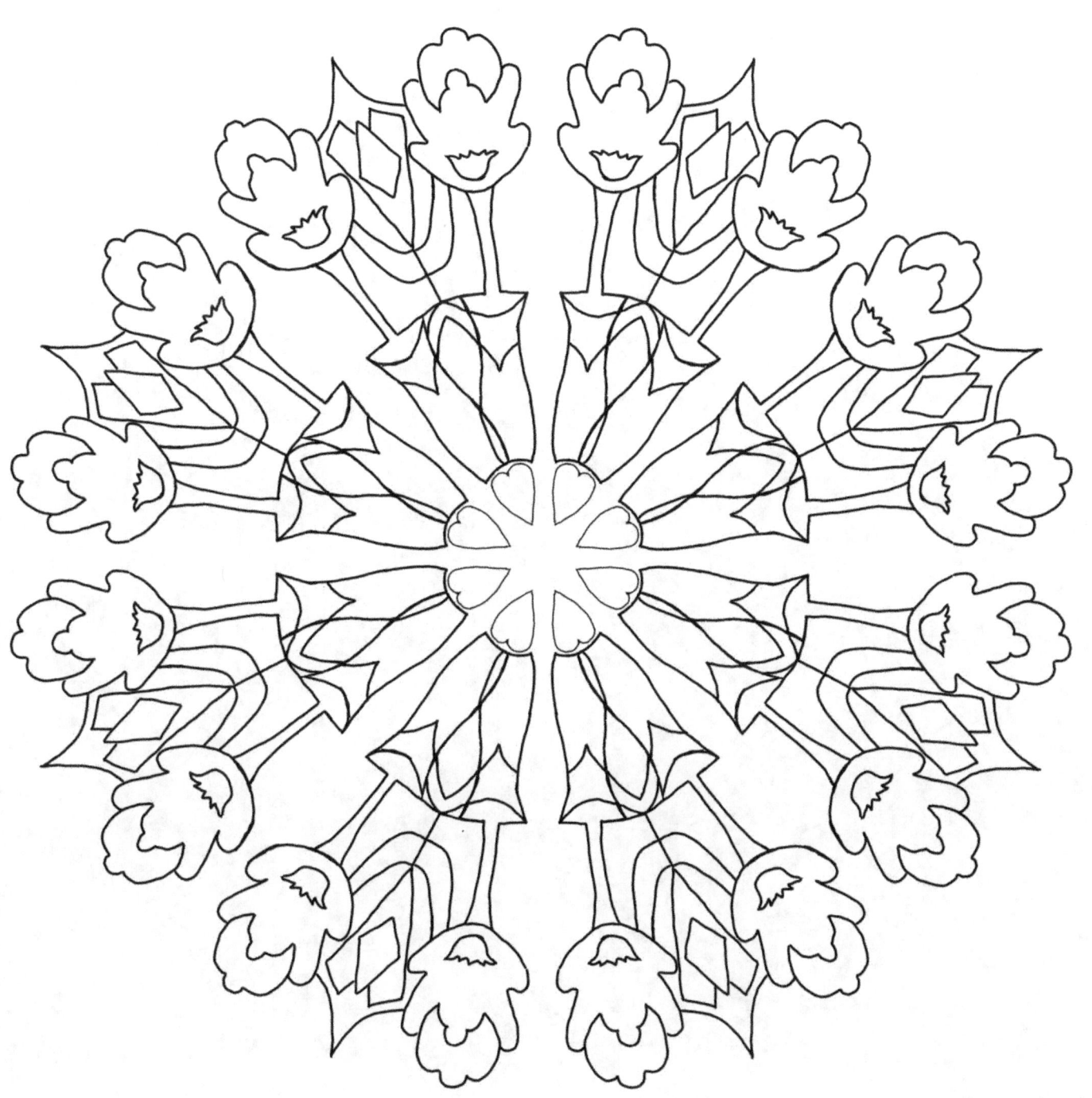

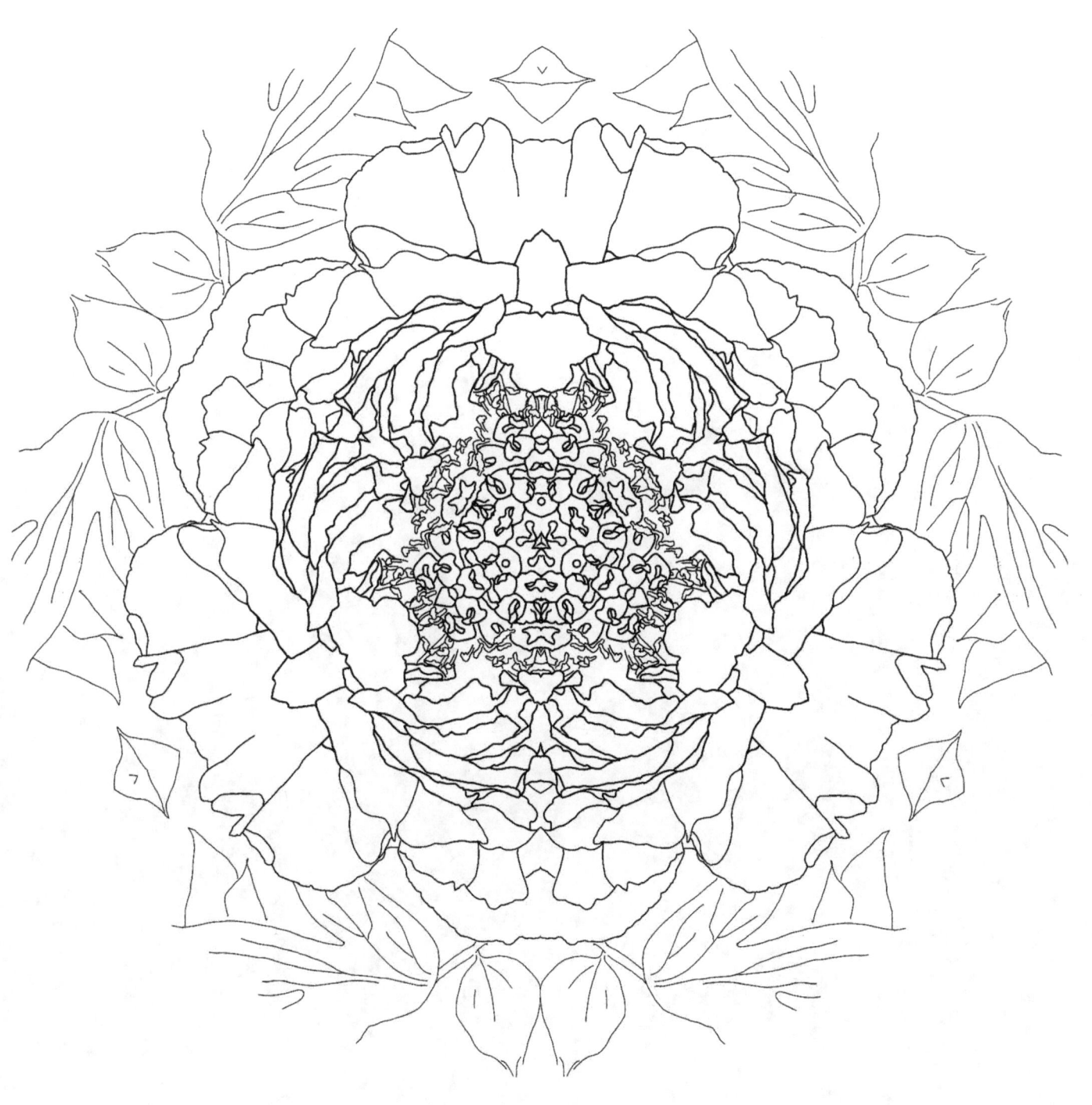

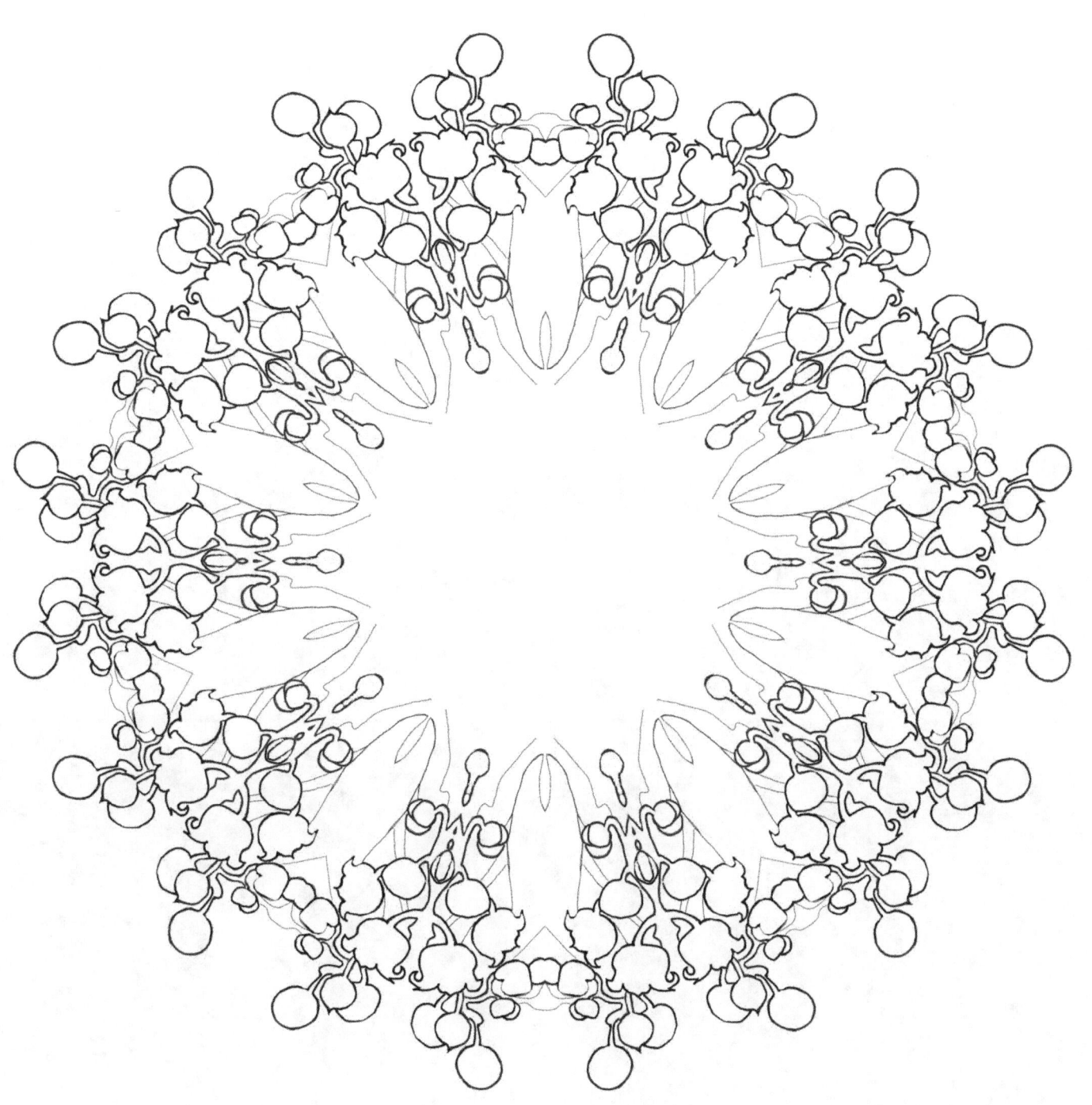

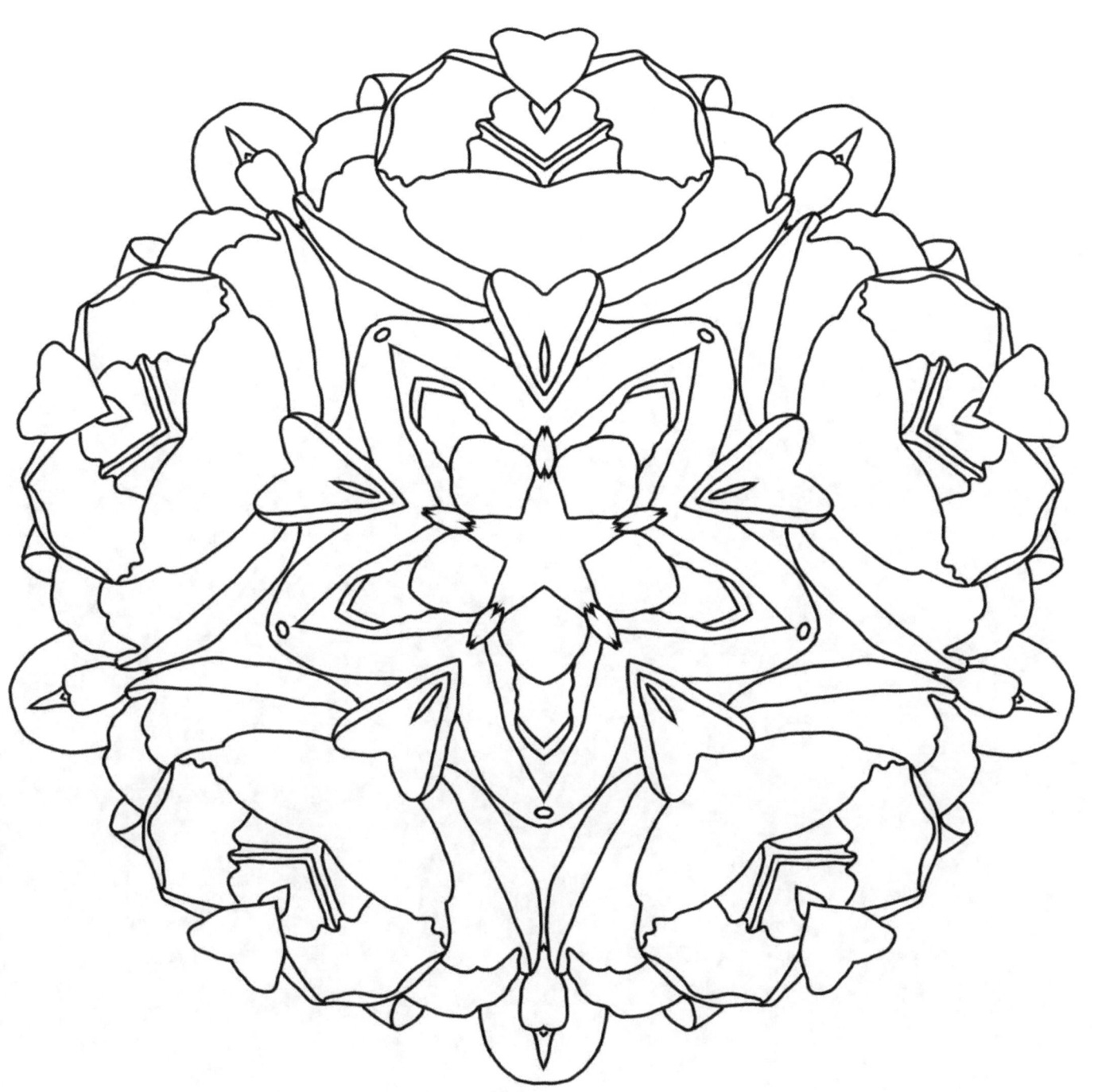

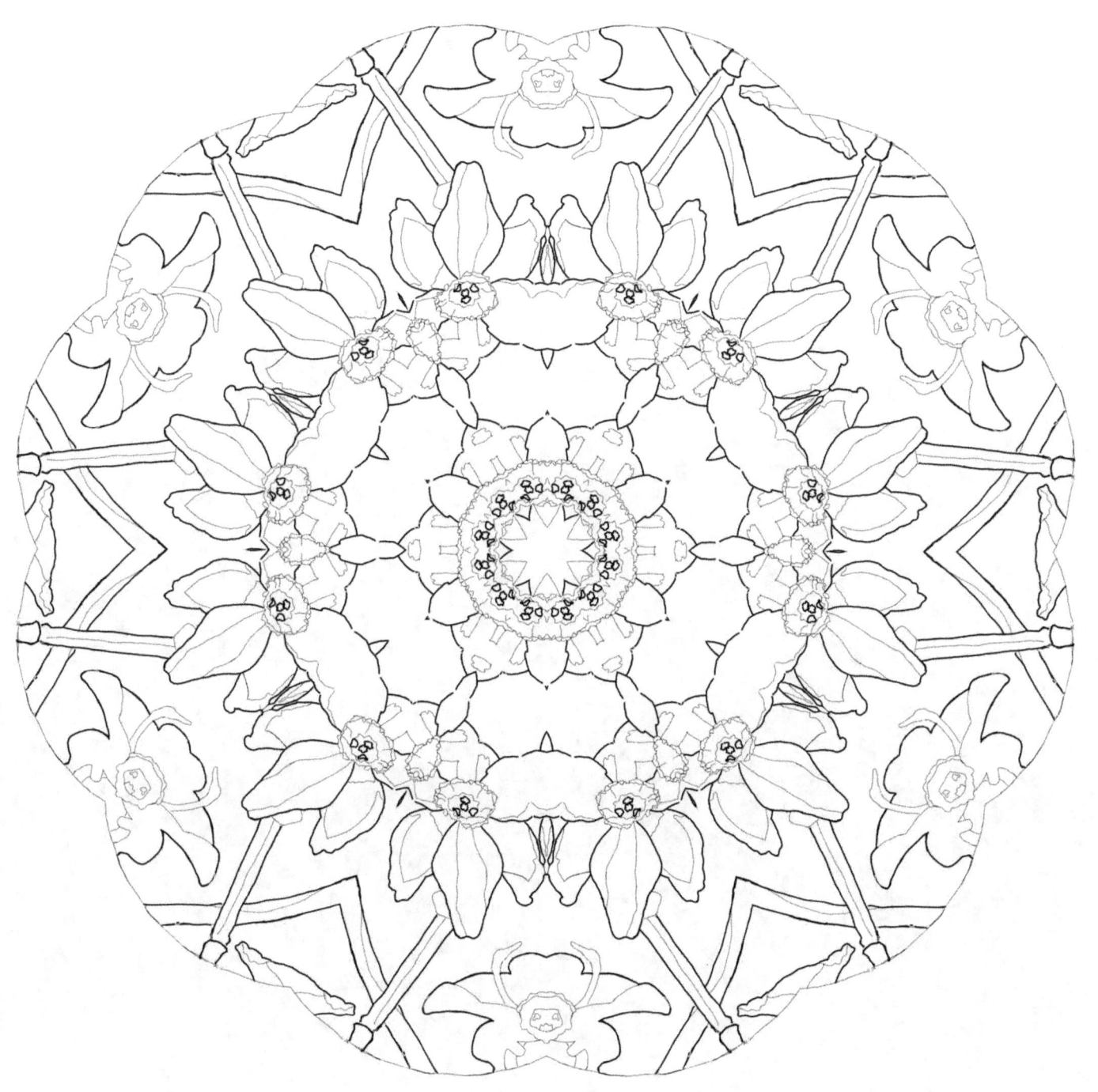

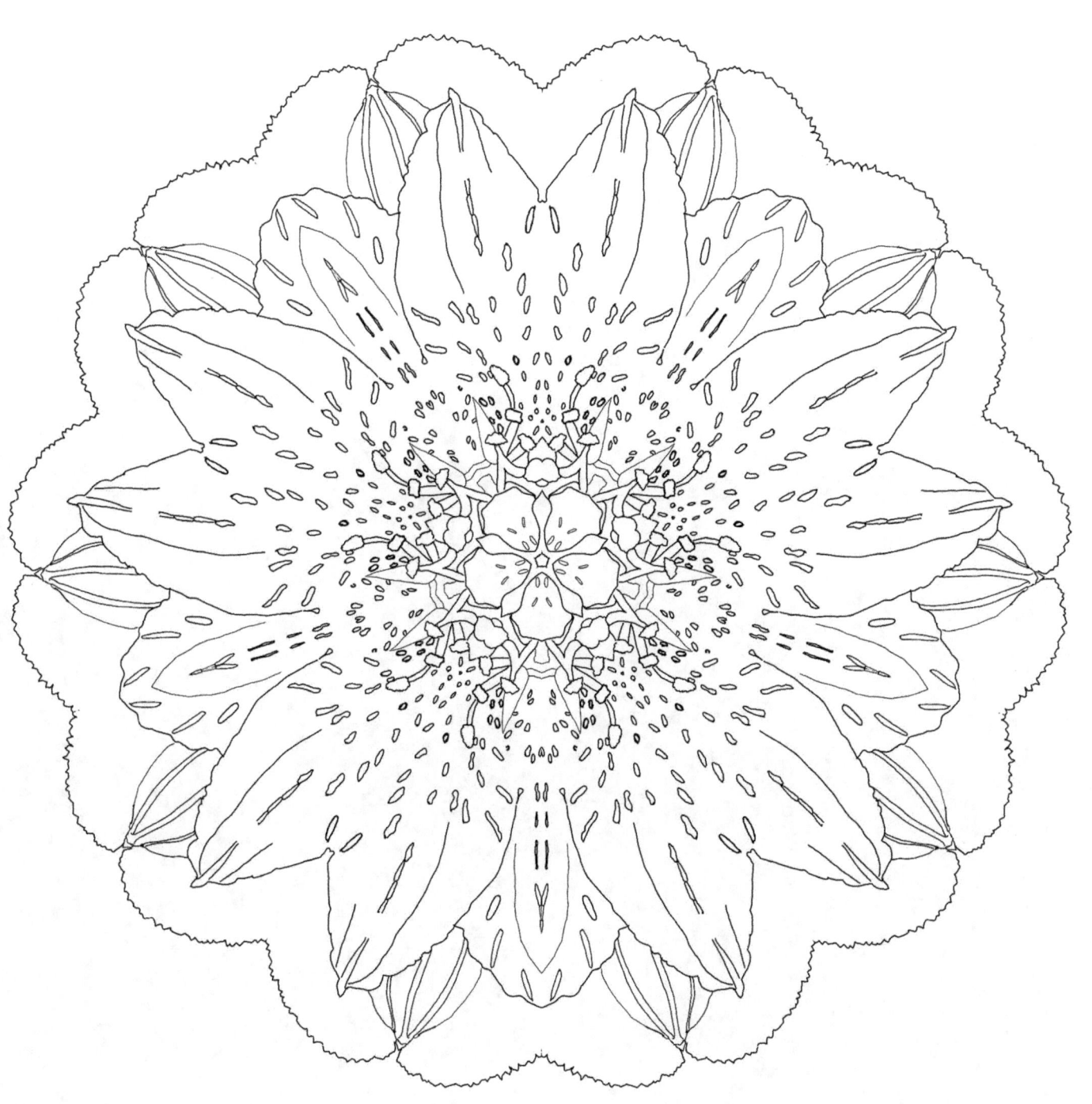

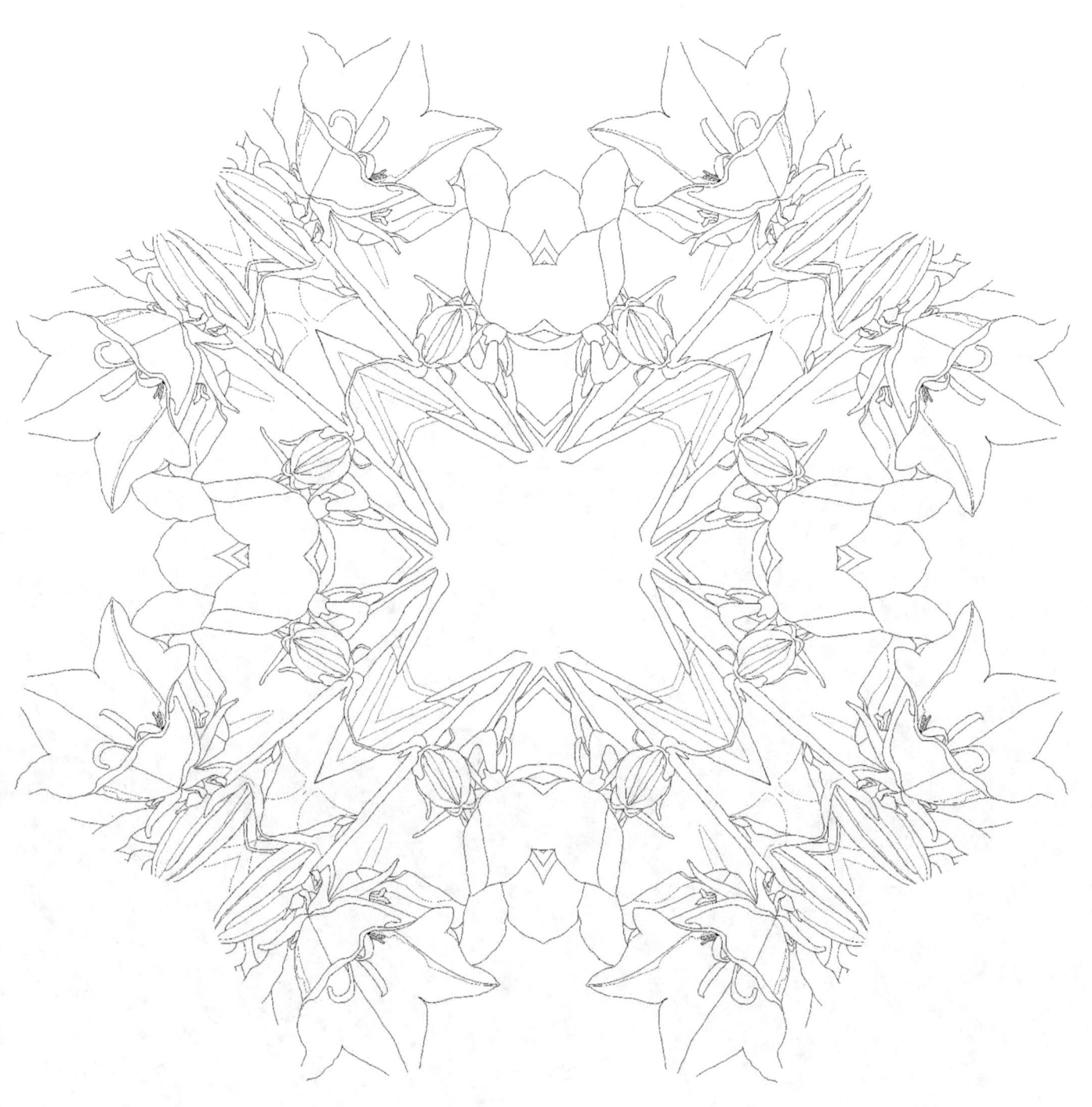

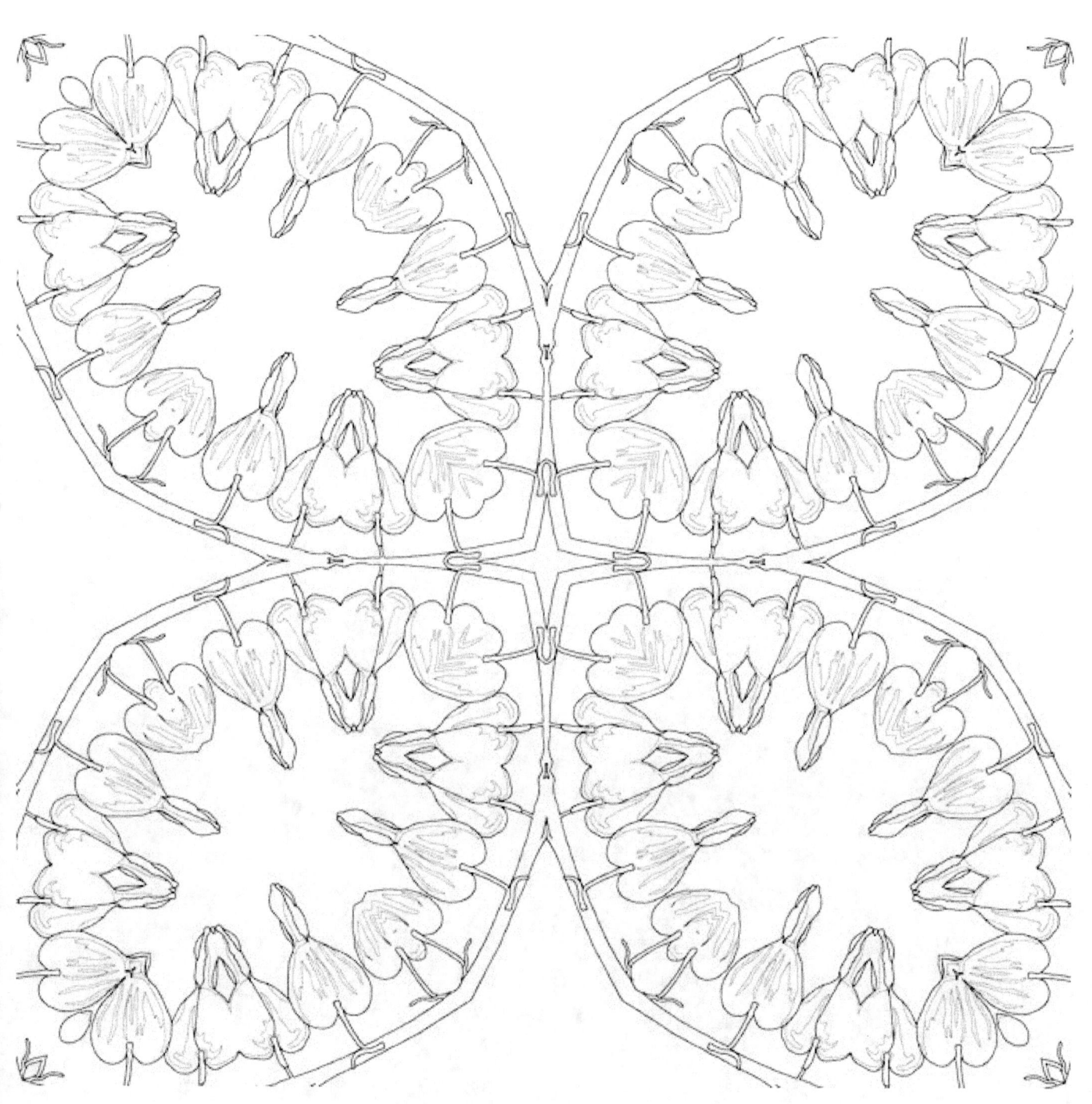

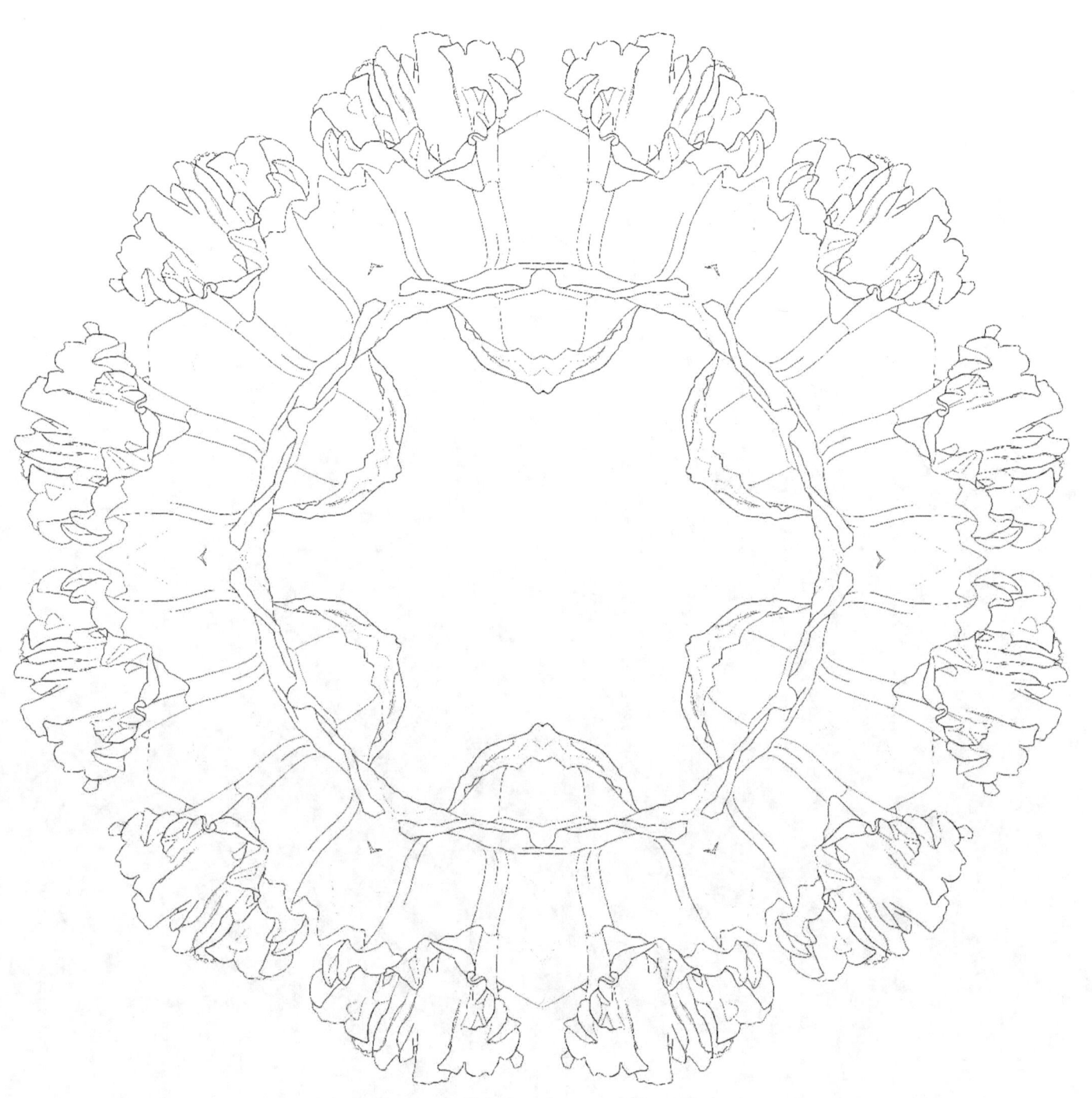

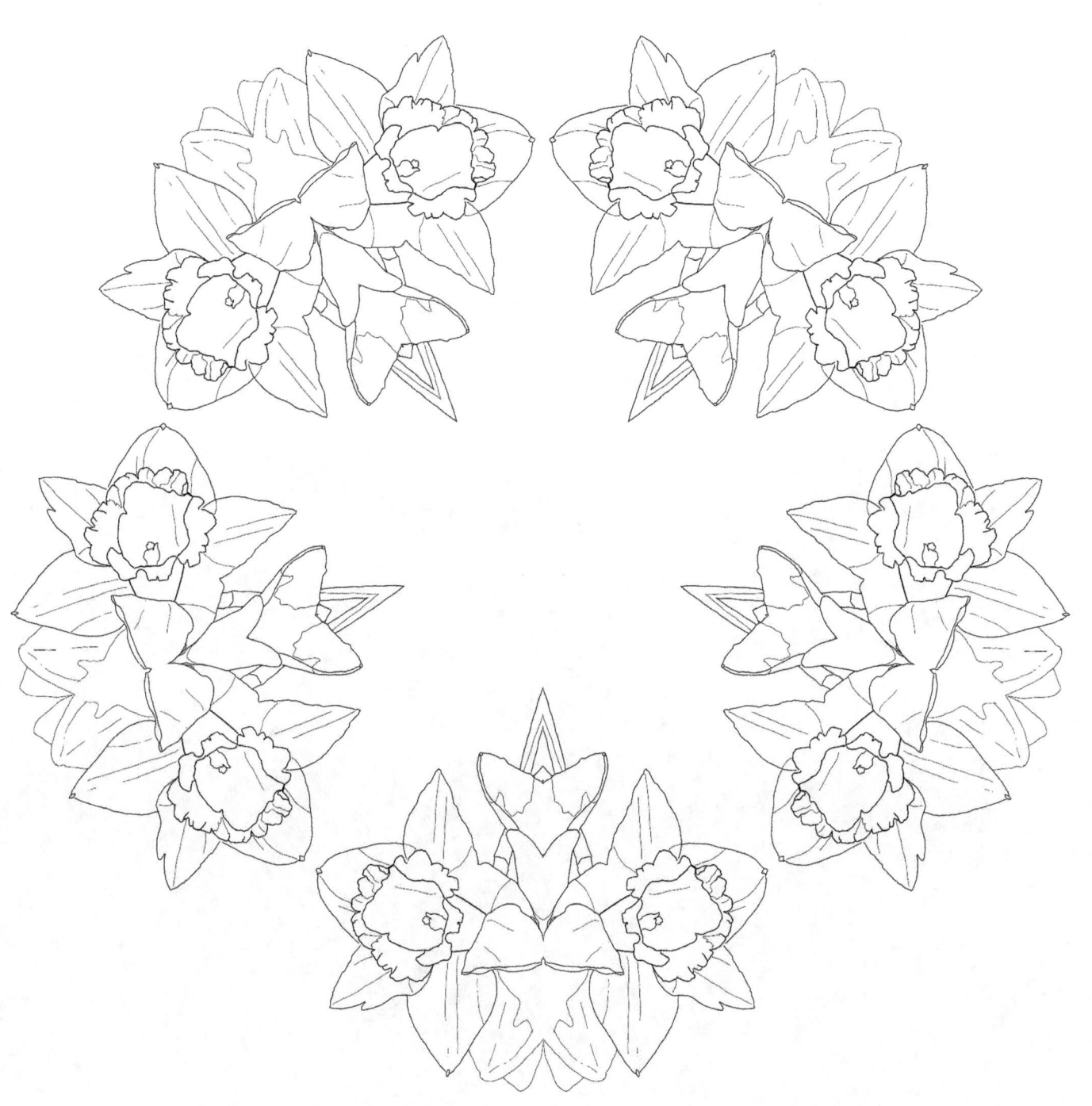

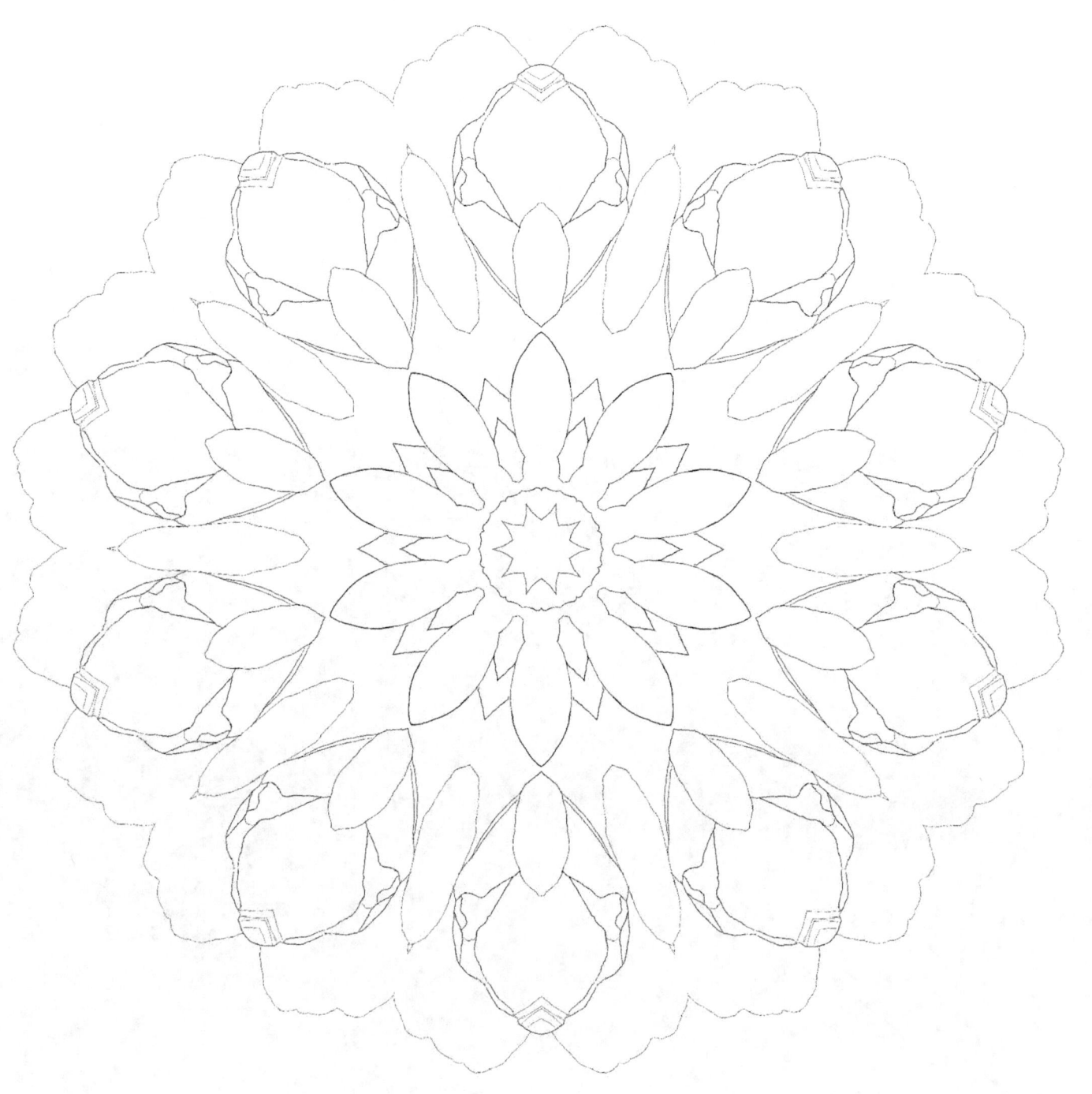

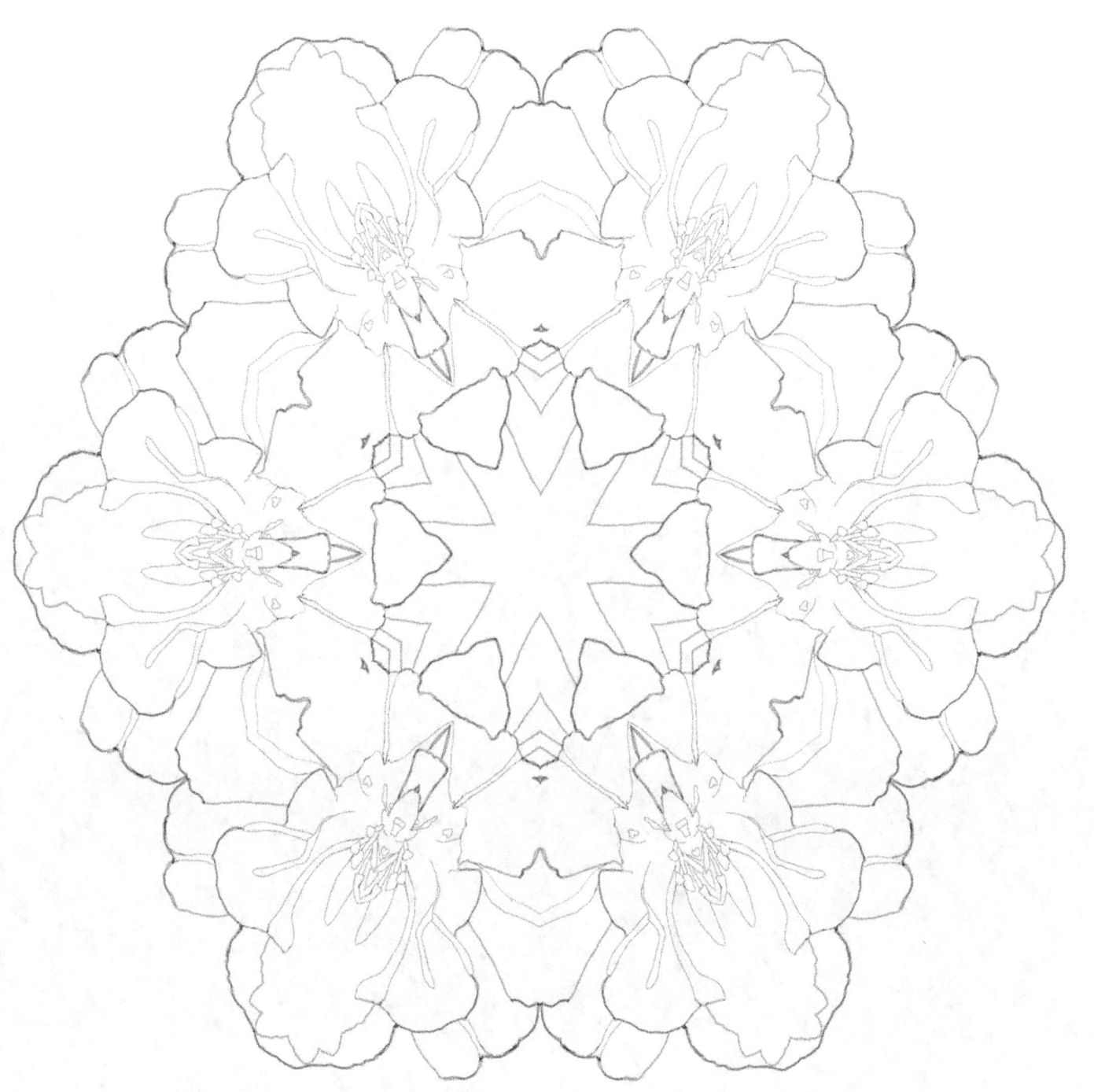

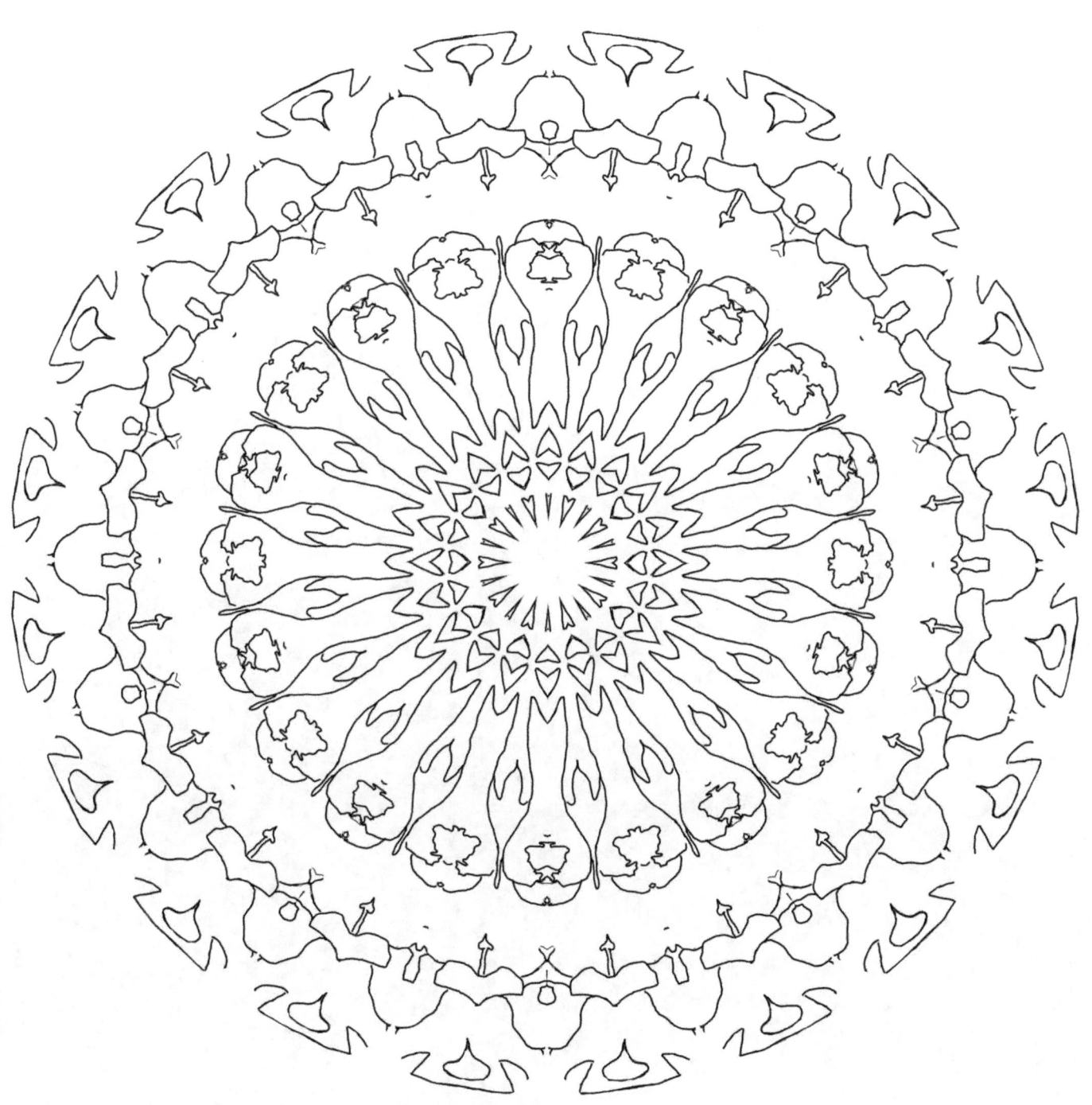

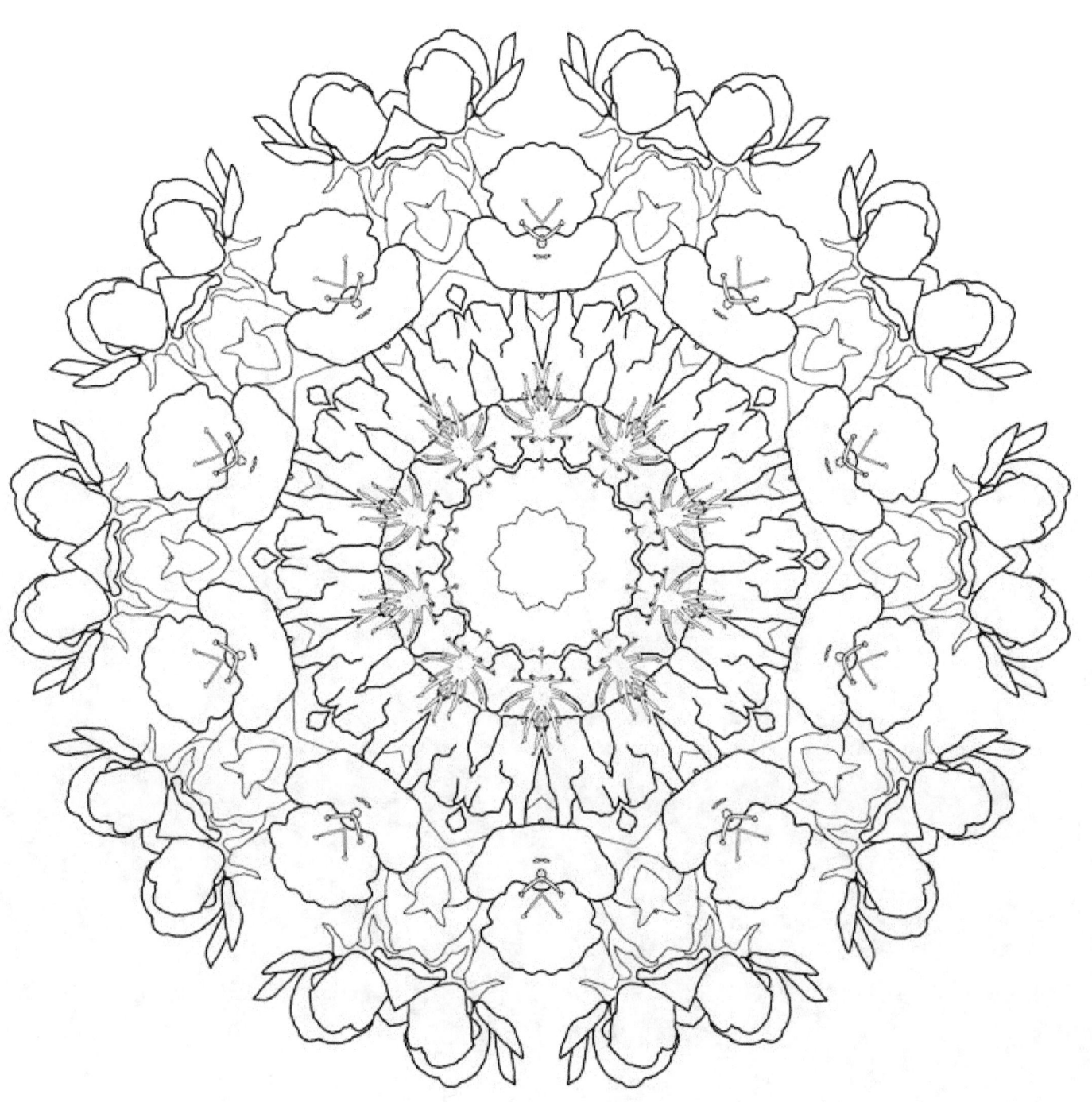

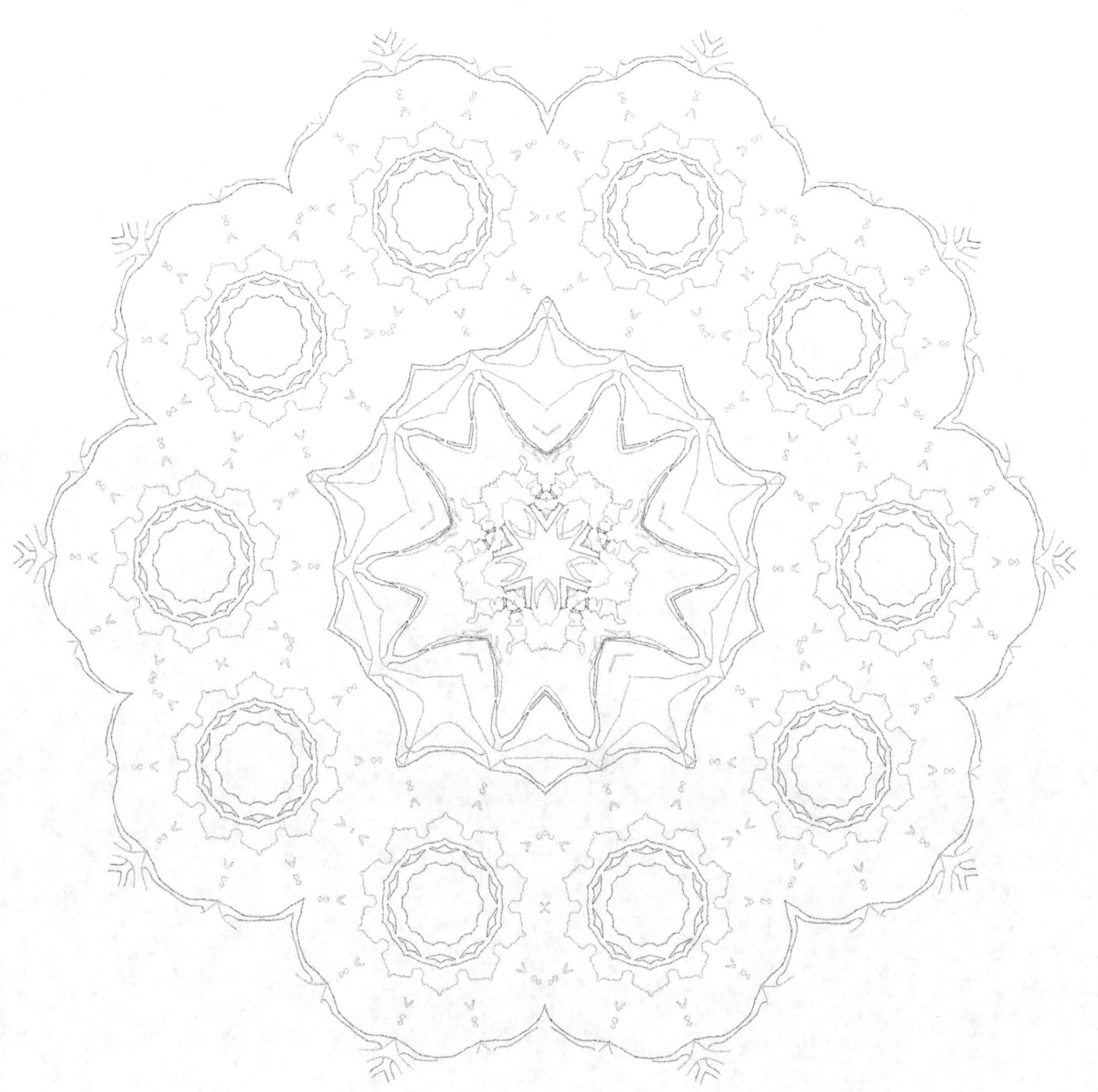

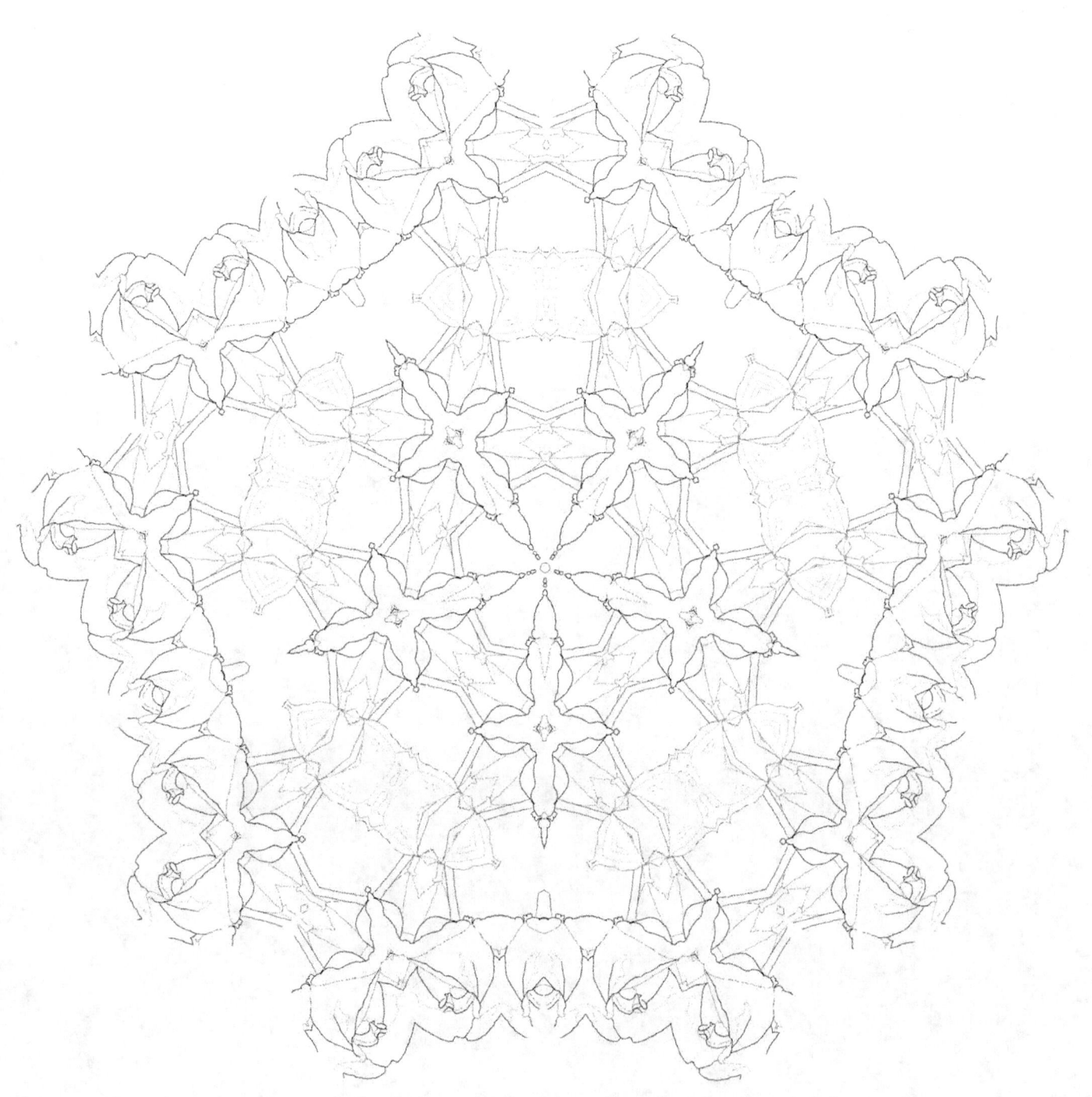

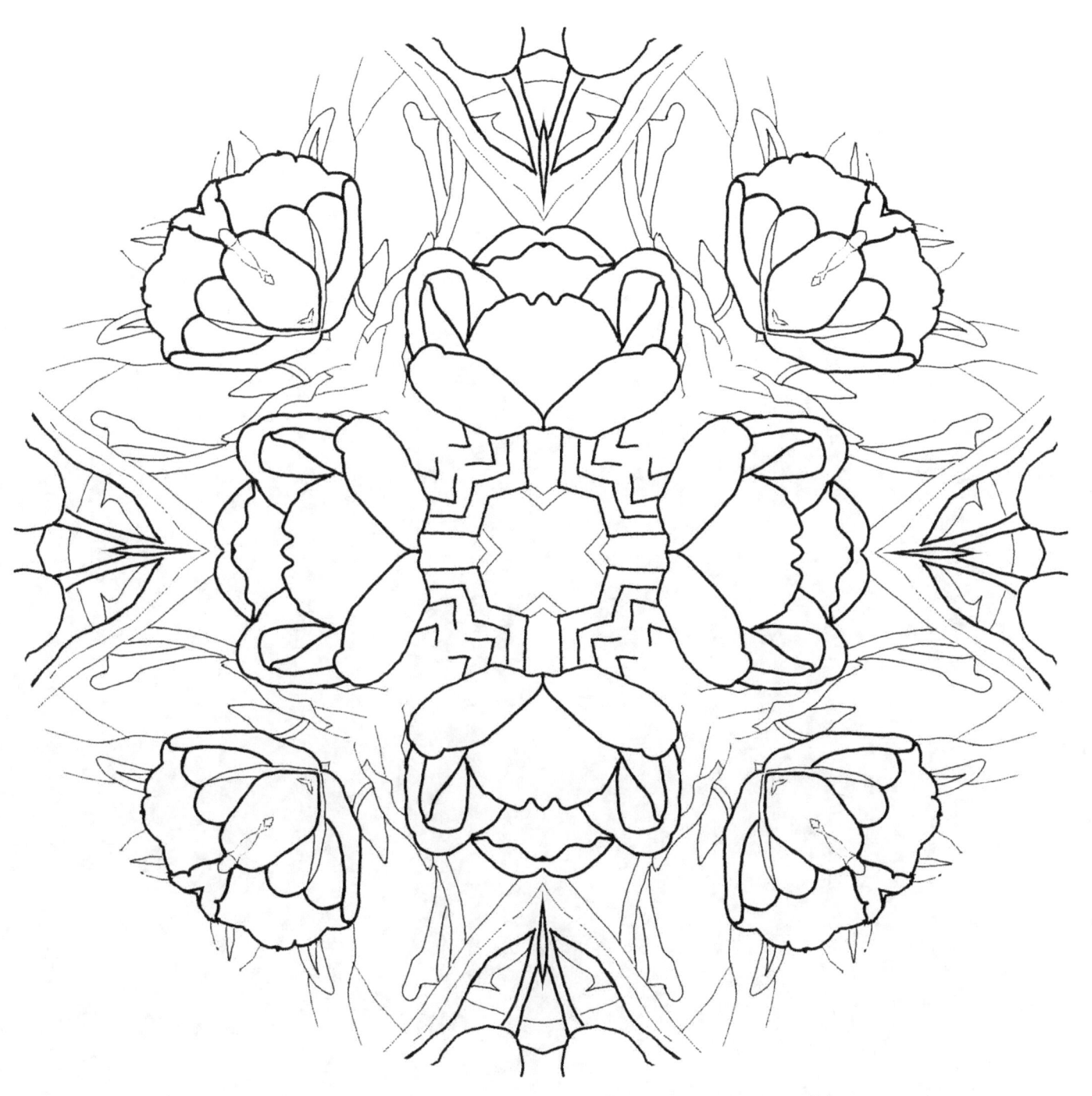

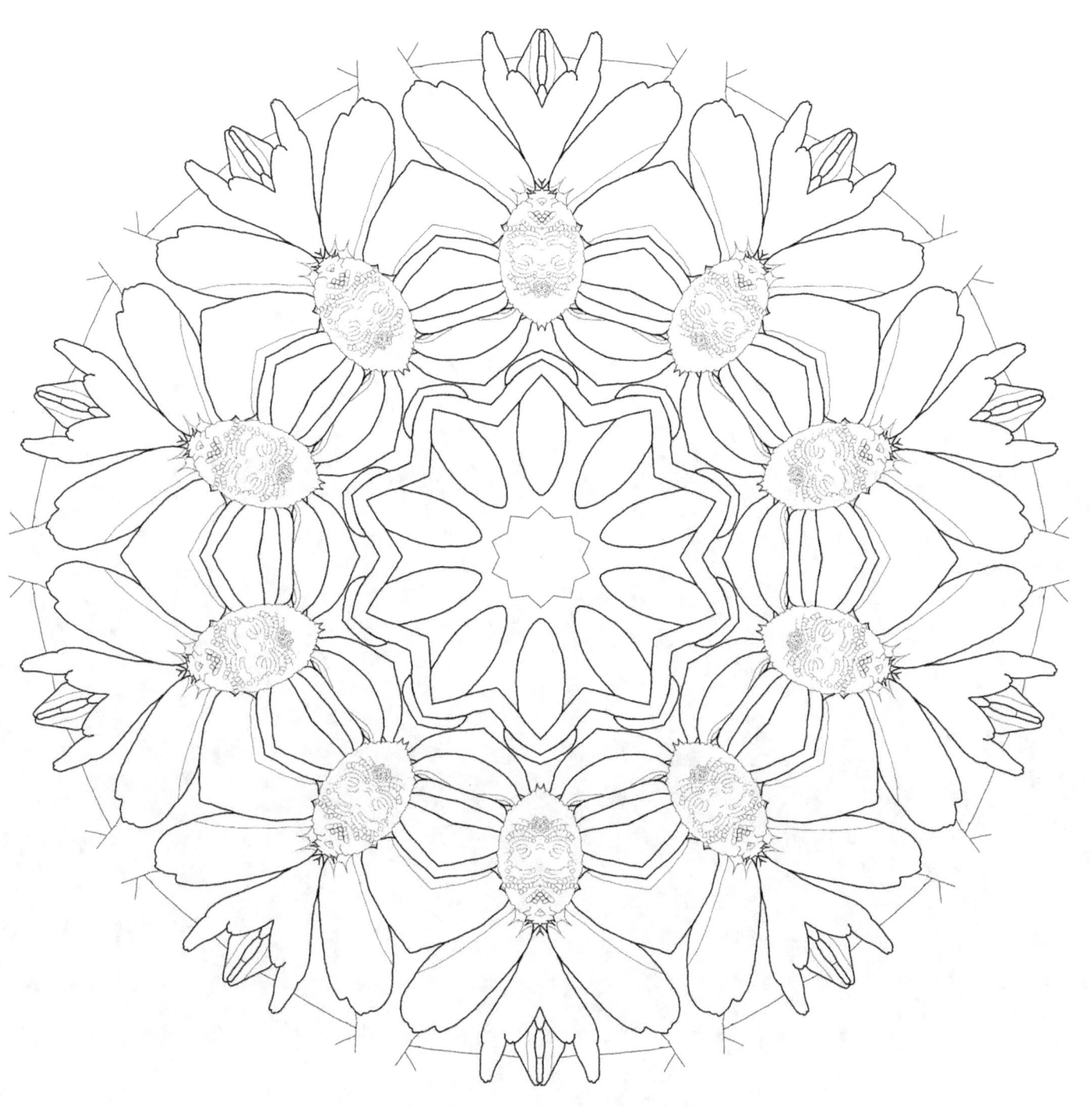

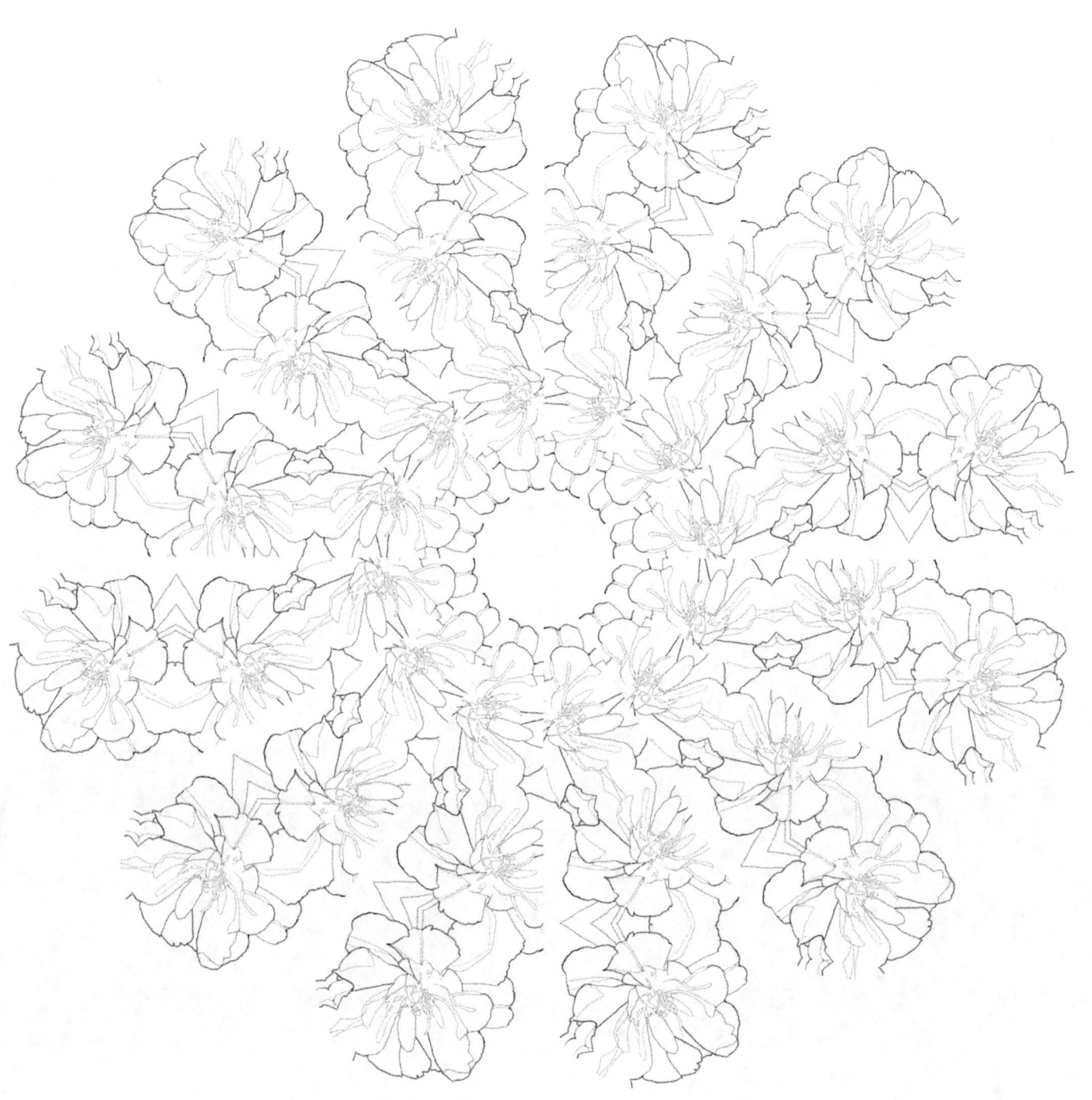

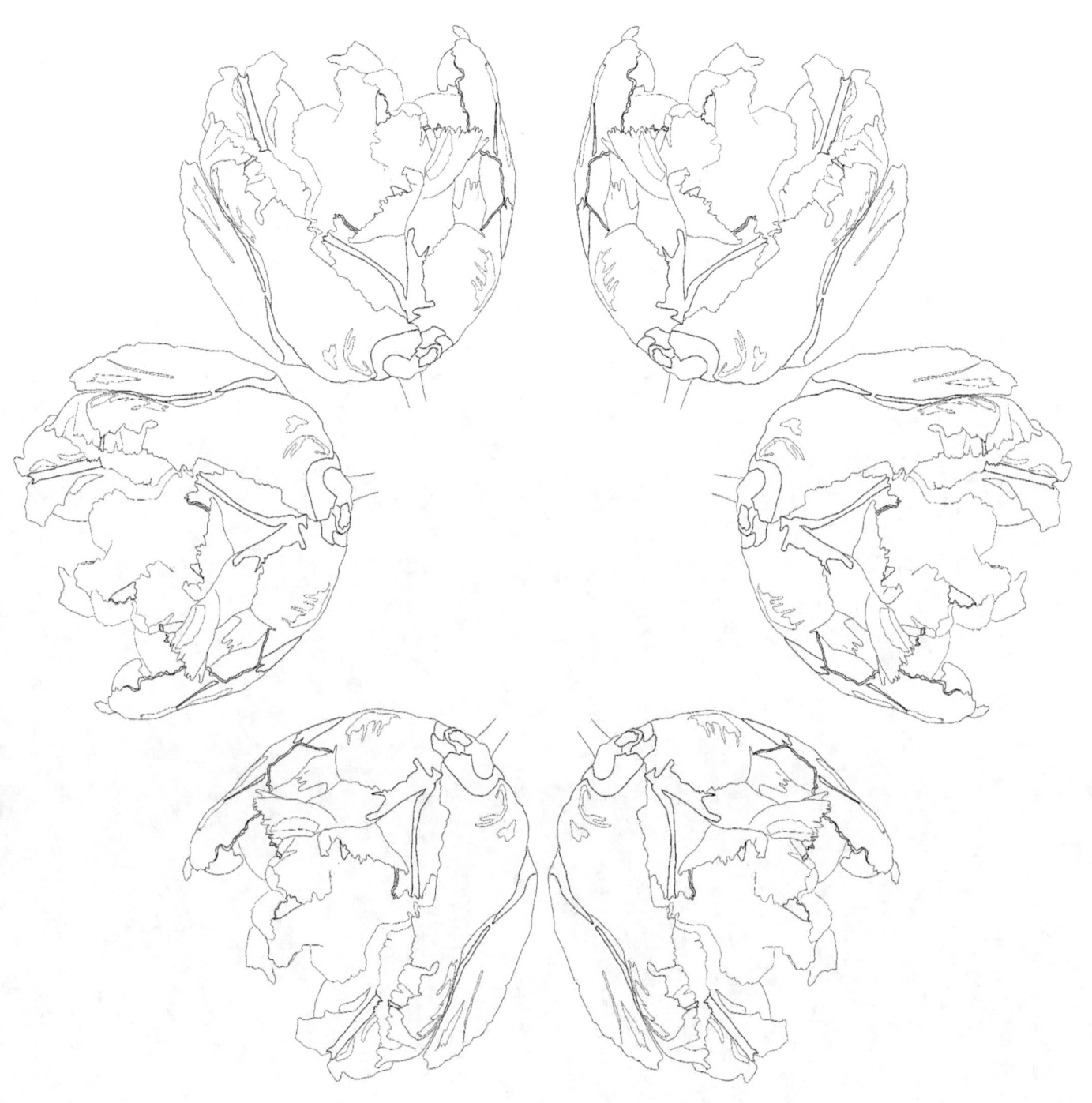

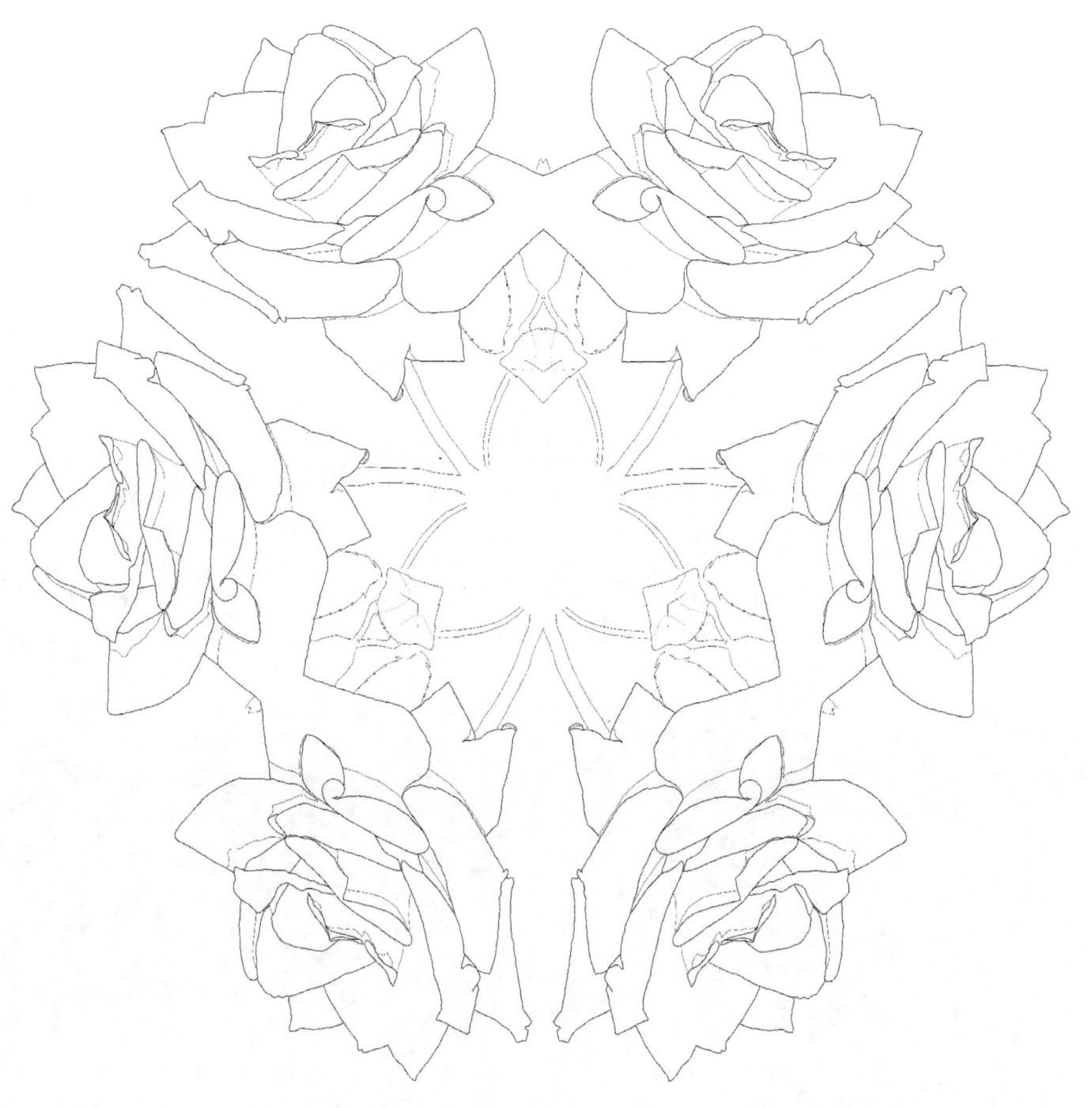

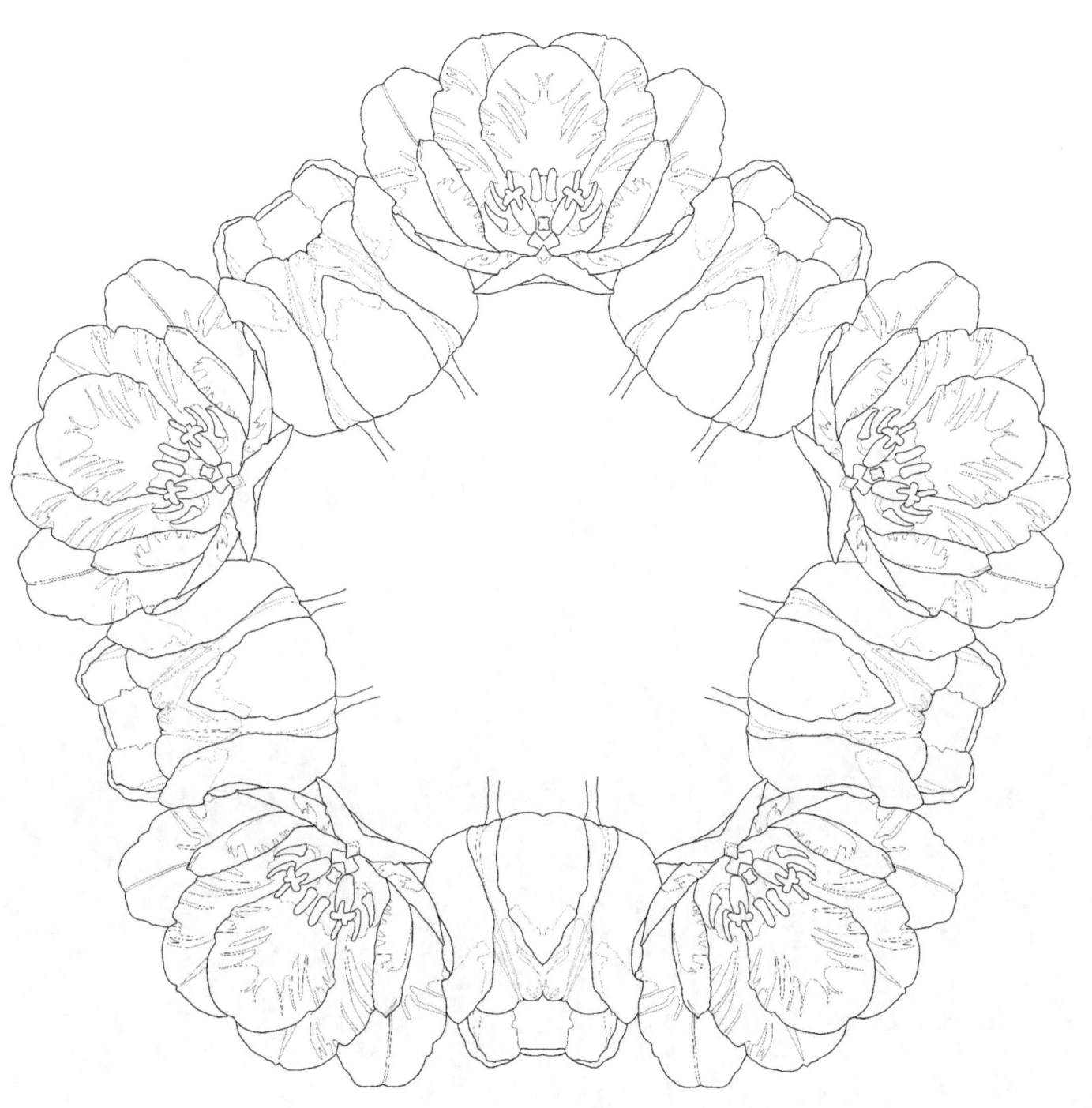

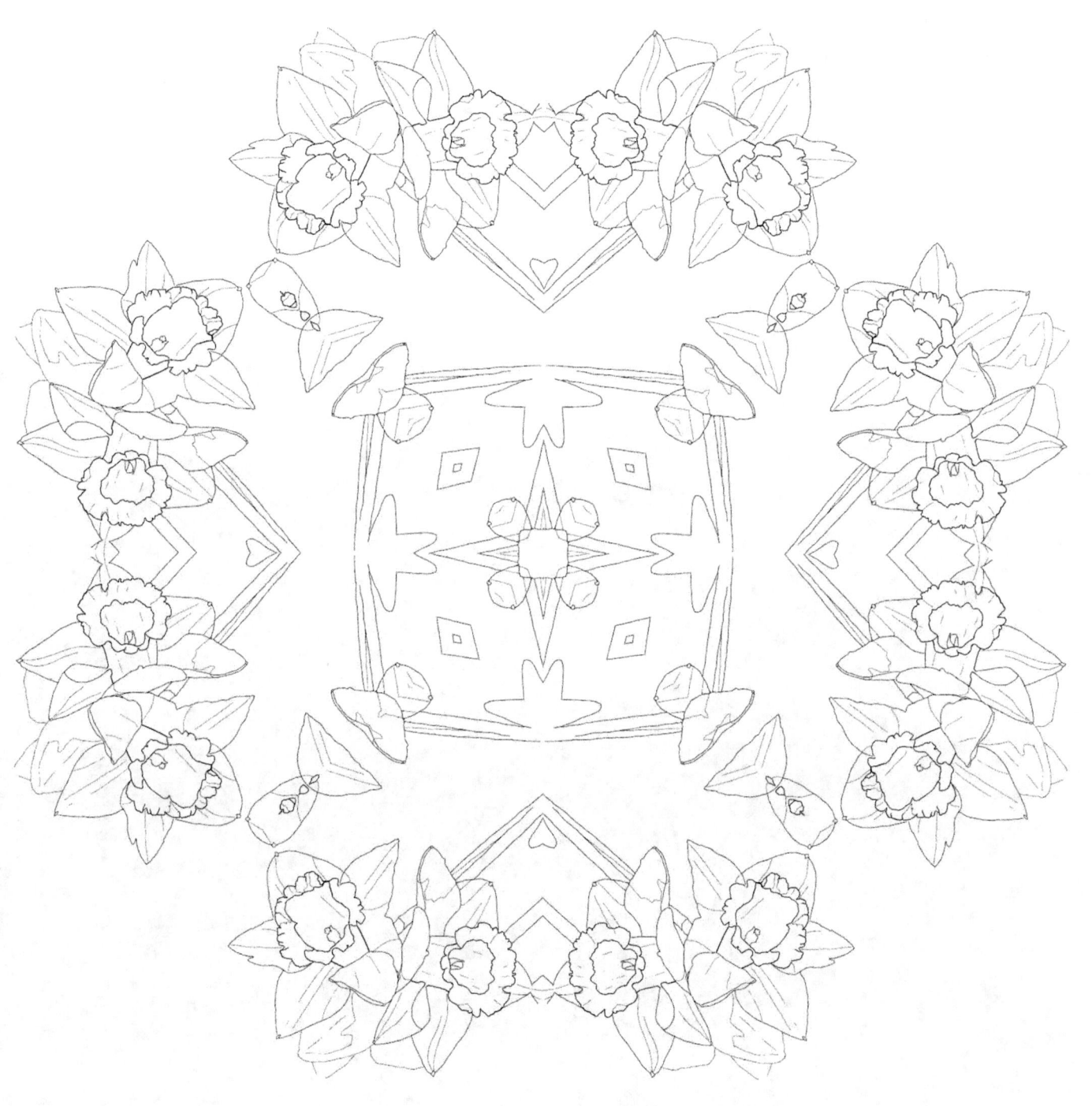

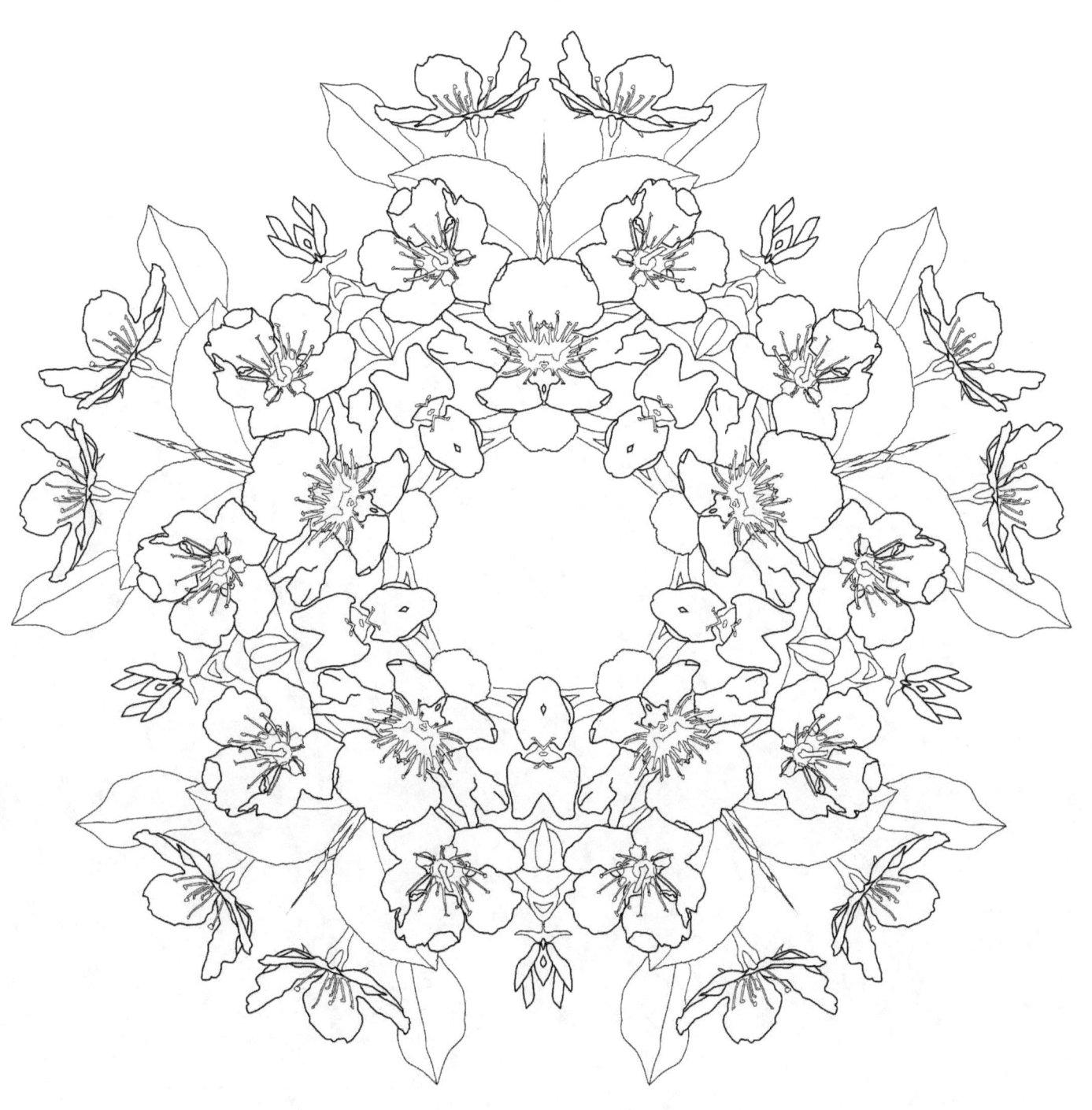

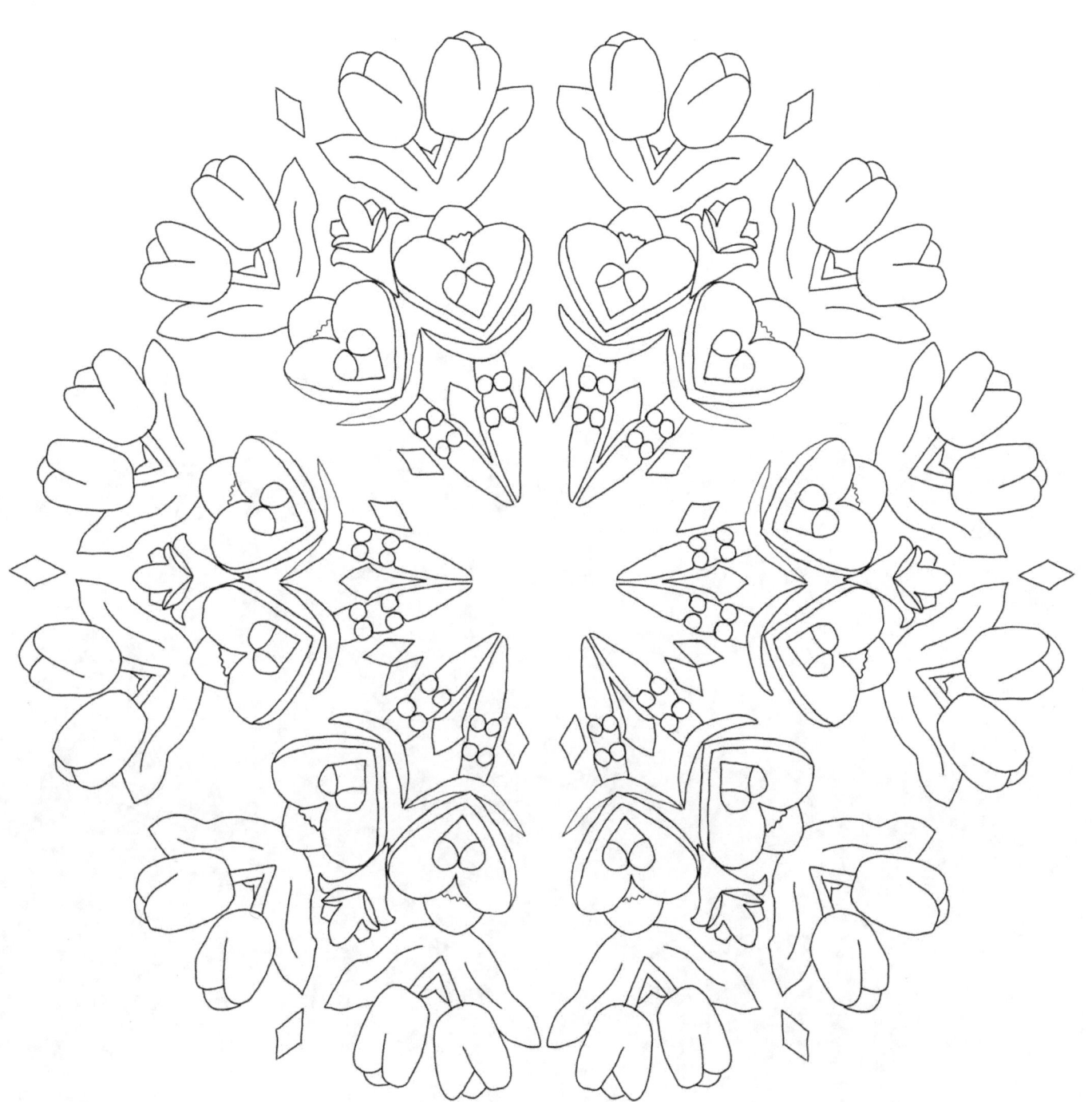

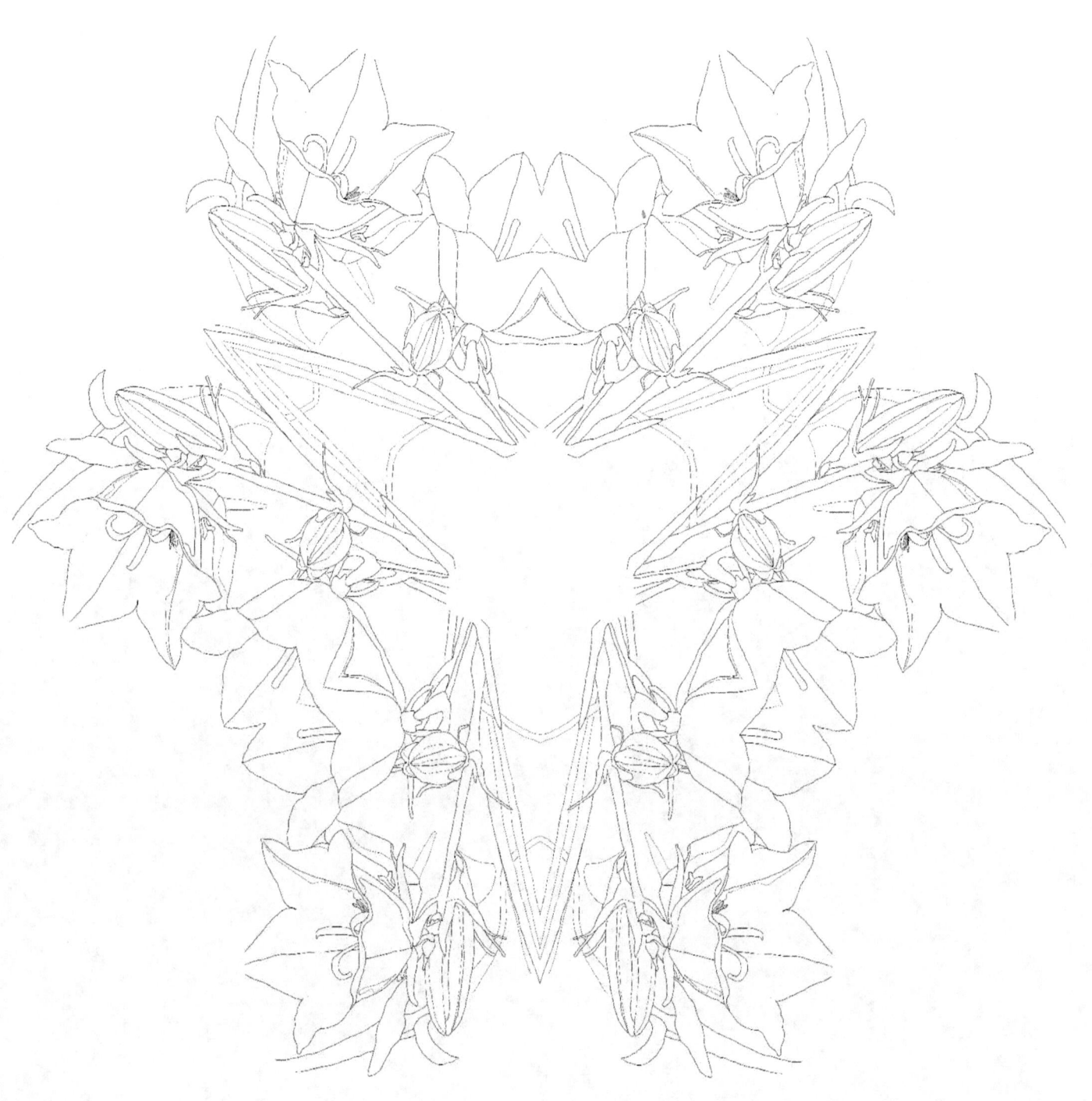

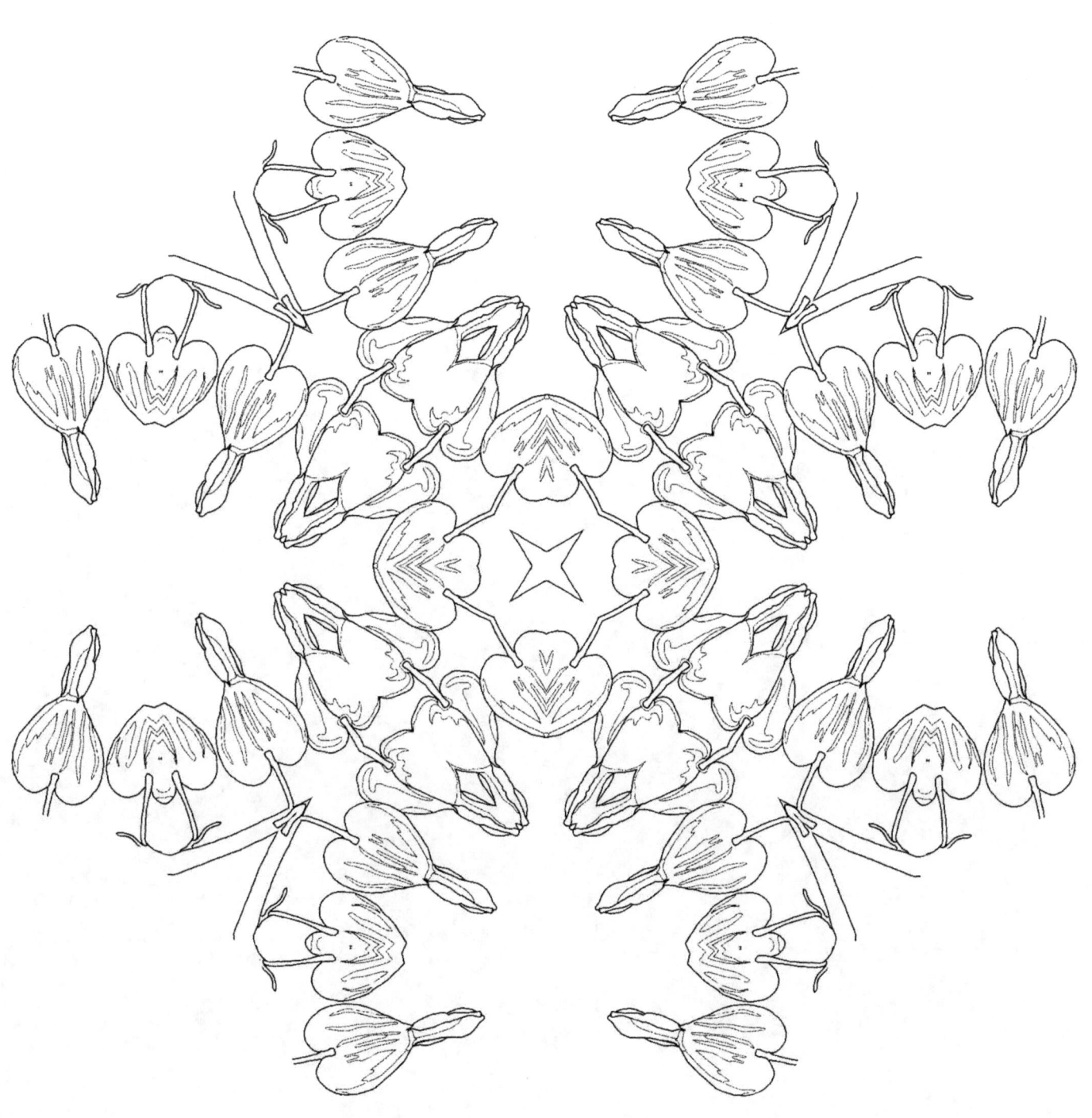

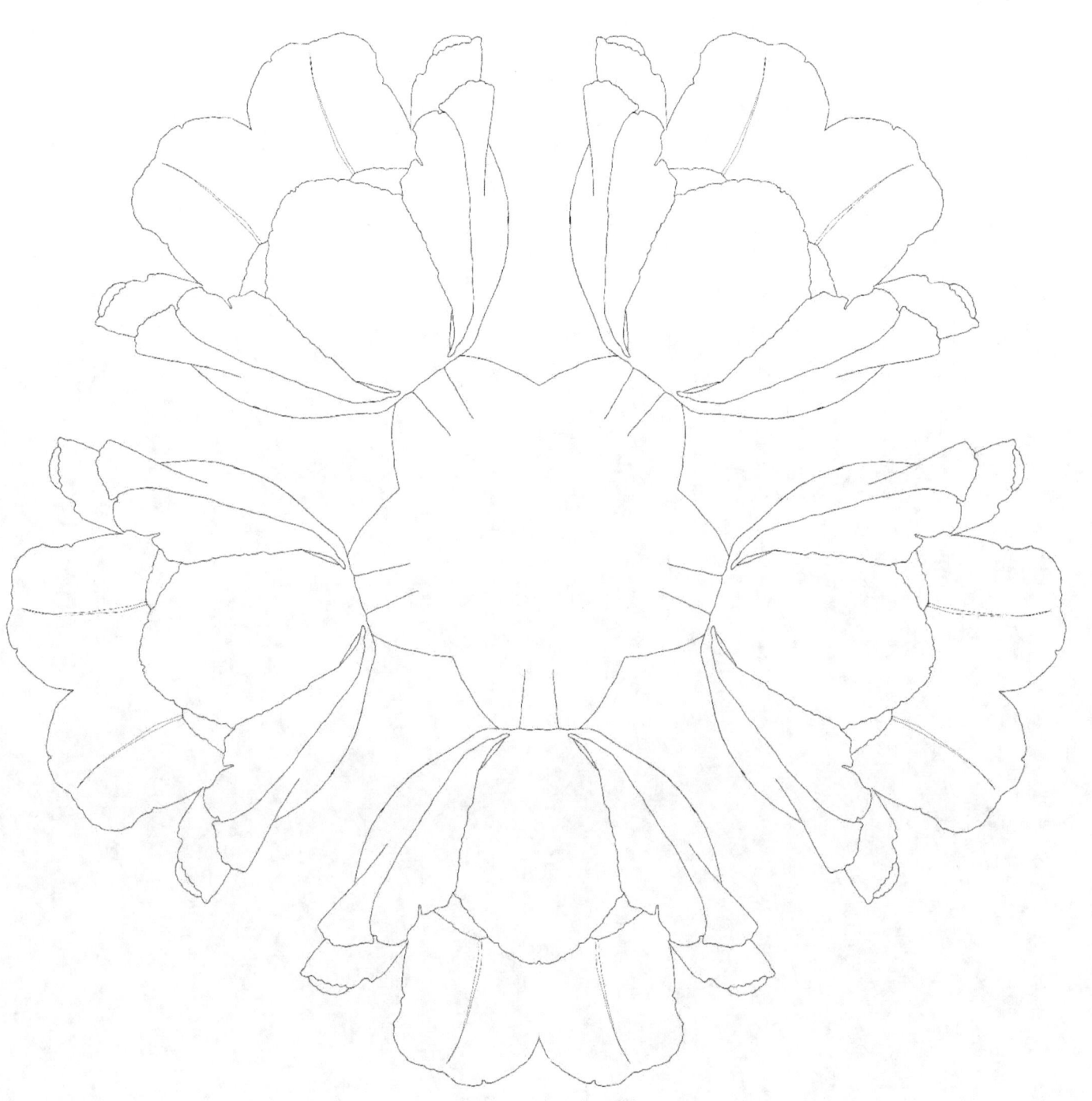

www.ingramcontent.com/pod-product-compliance
Lightning Source LLC
Chambersburg PA
CBHW080605180526
45168CB00007B/2788